Phosphorescence
of Thought

PETER O'LEARY

Phosphorescence

of Thought

THE CULTURAL SOCIETY

LOOKED AT IN ONE WAY, NATURE . . . IS A PENETRATING
SUMMONS TO THE SLOW EFFORTS, PATIENT AND UNSEEN, BY
WHICH THE INDIVIDUAL, HIMSELF BORNE ALONG BY A WHOLE
PAST, HUMBLY PREPARES A WORLD HE WILL NEVER KNOW.

Pierre Teilhard de Chardin
TO MARGUERITE TEILLARD-CHAMBON
JULY 27, 1915

FOR John Tipton

LOGONAUT

Phosphorescence

of Thought

T he wren

the mind

allows

to sing

alights

—and flits—

on branches bare

of anything other than the sun's ceaseless iodine

the woods at dusk flood with

like sutras meditators seep their thoughts in

neurochemicals recall from the galaxy's

antique axiometry. Alongside,

the Des Plaines River folding creamy gray through the trees bubbles

with pungent yeasts emplumed

in cottony lutrid foam engineered by

embankments men pile up

to keep

the river

tame.

The mind.
The mind assuming
reality. The mind's field of forces, its fluid exuberance
rebeginning, leaping up, folding back
into terminal unities endlessly

varying.
Cluster. Synthesis. Network. Node.
Centration.
The re-entering mental impulse.

The herring gulls circling; their yellow
gapes, the little crimson dots—breeding season. The mallards.
Their rotating strokes around the whirls, dabbling. Those lurid,
irisized heads.

Lutrid. Lutrescent. That's the mind's
excessive novelty, a tool preposterously ductile
language—pulling sound, image, light fluidly together—
freely commandeers
to feel reality,

to imagine light
gone rotten.

The wren,

        again.

A house wren. Its beak a slightly silvered sickle, its remembered song
—rapidly rolling, a bubbling, liquid trill—
an outlandish complexity copied
inventively from an adult
—a male—
not his father. A descending chirruping, a
draining descant he daylong intones variously, marking
the little log he's nesting in.

To begin.

The woods. The shabby little Forest Preserve.
The swerve of its trashy paths. The partying in its clearings.
The little house wren in it, his cinnamon supercilium, the drab
pattern of his plumage. And his mate—their clutch
of seven bean-sized eggs, luminously
speckled, hidden
deep in a cavity cleaned

from inside the fallen
log. The red-headed woodpeckers,
the flickers—darts defying gravity, their malars'

neon slash—the red-bellied *picadus*,
its deeply undulating flight. The avian cocaine
I take him for.

What
evolutionary acquisition does
that vibrant red
express? And what

do I love in loving thee?

lumen de lúmine
Deum vero de Deo vero; génitum
non factum, consubstantialem Naturæ; per quam
omnia facta sunt.

With the oldest cherubim of knowledge,
the phanophagous cherubs, devouring
with their bodies the light they transform into scissoring flame
flared forth sword-like and brandished, unspeakably
world-like, fully
recklessly
imagined.

We now begin our study of the mind
within. Let us use the words *psychic overtone,
suffusion,* or *fringe.*

Let us
speak in whispers of the one,
of the meticulous hinge
on the Book of Knowledge hidden
in rapt

prelude. Apart. Come.

Let us use the word *re-entry.*
Let us sing the differentiating motions
whereby thought's signals
slide in runnels
down the mind's
great glacial expanse

pooling
at the base, lubricating
its massive shelves, its agonized
calves. Let us use

the word *epistrophe*
to mean the turning back of otherwise organized energy
to the supra-organized
diadem of the Godhead—premeditative acts
of prayer. Pre-

cognitive flights of birds.

   The warbler
the oriole
the blackbird
the bunting.
   The sparrow
the waterthrush
the warbler
the wren.
   The wren
the hermit thrush
the warbler
the redstart.
   The yellowthroat
the sparrow
the kinglet
the kestrel.

The hawk
the wren
the kestrel
the cranes.

: :

The great glorious anteceding mind bent
to tell
of shapes transformde to bodies straunge.

Before the sea
and before the lands
and before the omnium of the sky overhanging

Nature
was an unatomized sundering of sames: called

chaos—

a rude huge heap unordered and ill-fitted, a clotted
discordion of seeds squeezed elementally in a premonitional junctrix.
No sun.
No shining forth. No
moon.
No horns repaired with borrowed
light. No air

circumfused with light. No sweet earth
perfectly pendant, bright,

no ocean with tensing arms embracing the earth about.

God made this, composed it.
God tore land from sky, sea from land
secreting from airy heavens the liquid
days, the atmosphere
they slide through . . .

In dissociating the massive blind heap of things—concordia, peace.
    The elements
into their vast realms settled. Fire
actively expelling matter weightlessly
rose up
igniting heaven's convex
lens, its winking arch. Nearer to us is the air, levitating
in place. Gravity's pressing density, telluric and grand, tracks earth
to the bottom of the heap. Coerced circumfluidity
solid masses get overrun by
makes the rivers with endlessly streaming waters
that power the weather's elements
flow.

    : :

Excentration.

Divergence, distribution. Transverse being,

transverse reality. Atoms. Grains. Corpuscled.

Particles, bits, specimens, fragments. Elements.

Stock, swarm, series, whole, phalanx. The elements of the whole

may be enumerated exhaustively. Numerousness.

Abundance, proliferation: nature: the world: the universe: the cosmos: degrees

of reality. From matter through accidents to truth.

The apex. The spiritual focus of the ellipse of the real. Biosphere. Noosphere.

   Christosphere.

Force: energy. Field of forces. Impetus. Dynamism.

Tension, propulsion, urge, impulse; current (maelstrom);

countercurrent. Fluid, flux, influx, efflux. Tide.

Flow. Ebullition.

Profusion, exuberance, effervescence.

Attack. Combat. Repugnance. Spur.

Paroxysm. Apotheosis. Stop.

Exhaustion. Catastrophe, shipwreck of the singular, condemnation, check,

route, miscarriage, dead-

end.

Rebeginning.

Leap. Resurrection. Recasting. Renewal.

The progress of the unity in forms.

The increase in unification.

The impulse of elementary and imperfect unities.

Through complexity toward an absolute

Terminal

Unity.

An organized whole in the process of fulfillment.

Complexity. Centration. Convergence. Confluence. Coalescence.

Concrescence; compression, folding back, condensation;

infolding, interpenetration; bond, cementation;

fusing, knot, buckle, attachment, linking, fascicle;

corpusculization, moleculization, planetization, constellation.

Junction, adhesion, connexion,

agglutinization, cluster.

Synthesis.

Form, stuff, tissue, texture, braid, stitch.

Anastomosis. *Network*. Procession.

Integration, consummation, completion.

The transparence of God in the universe.

The heights where God dwells not an inaccessible mountain but a profounder
sphere of things.

— : —

Creation is humans' memory system. Cranes
rely on magnetic streams
to remember. Sparrowhawks

on superaccurate eyesight—light's flickering peripheries
patterned out as
tiny rodent motion. Their hovering is still; their stooping
soundless.

       Kestrel:
its evidence is the air's, that autochthonomous unearthing,
unleashing aerobatics to hover lustrously in a wind-groomed leewave.
That's air's predatory excesses trimmed

into an evolutionary
leanness.

That's the sun's own *killy-killying* carapace.

What's it like to be a falcon?
As strange as being a man, and
as idiomatic—.

It's more owl than hawk.
More wisdom than war.
More hovering wind than merciful mind.
More mind than mentation.
More massively reentrant than speciously reentrancing.

More richly environmental than metaphorically unitary.
More autochthonomously unleashing than
through the void plummeting.
More splendidly envisioning than accident of life.
More gift than gall, more
phenomenal still. More like sleep rupturing waking than
like building a temple.
To coax the divine
in.

More like gaining altitude than boring through the earth.
More earth's
ward than
air's excess.

More binding and synchronous than operatively constructive.

                                              A kestrel
can resolve a minute insect by precisely
bobbing its head up and down, triangulating by parallax its fluttering
    position,
from twenty yards away. Its eyes
are so huge the back of each orb presses into
the middle of its skull, each the size
of a red grape.

Whose insides weirdly resemble the fruit's flesh—an
avascular retina in which neither shadow nor light-scatters
interfere with vision: one million cones, and each photoreceptive cell
directly represents its data in the brain. Imagine
the words of your thoughts dropping from your ears onto
the pavement, piled there.

You

have one fovea in each eye; falcons have two—these foveae fuse to produce
stereoscopic vision, field's depth in falconine
richness.

Where in humans vision is a sense,
in falcons vision is thought itself, the avian mind's ductile conversion
of reality into raptorial
being.

    Life's
most perfect instrument of vision
is a falcon's roving eye.

In barest functional terms, a kestrel
is a pair of eyes set in a well armed, exquisitely engineered
airframe. And there's a set of them, at the treetops seen
from the alley—a family?—resting in my
binocular focus.

The elm in mid-March. Leafless aureating circuitry against the sky.
Gray. Creamy. Along the branching aura's
underside, two raptors
at work, undistracted—at ease. A Cooper's hawk
feigning uncoordination, staggering
from one flimsy limb to a lower,

is operating actually—pulling
a twig from dead wood.
Expanding air, too warm so soon, feathers the elm
with silence

onto which the hawk trampolines,
swooping gently
quietly down

between houses to its alley
eyrie.

Alternately, a cool blue merlin
daubed dull in the low-
contrasting light grooms

its feathers, fretting them with air
in ruffed undulations as the merlin moves its

polished onyx beak in yogic
rotations from head to anus, gently nibbling
the uropygial gland preening
its wings' pulvered grooves with fatty acids the sun,
when it bursts out at last, will convert

into vitamin D. Perched there.

Upright, puffed from the work. Silent.

Its blue coloration common to raptorial bird-killers.

A kestrel soars, revolving the sky through the vanes of his wings.

Worship.
Veneration.

The little falcon's latriated flight.
The sparrowhawk's hyperduliated flight.
We shall see and we shall love. We shall love and we shall praise.
Involuntary light.
The glistening radiance—the vanity of the imagination.
The consuming fire sacrificial divinity is.

   : :

So earthly and ancient.

Precipitate of space, a streaking meteor carrying plutonic memory
its impact will unleash into act—exploded star, alchemy's enigma. Its
crypto-ecclesial vitriol. A *vox aeterna.* An azoic
vitalizing ash imagination concentrates. Alchemists
act as an aerolith's horoscope—stargazing
is fossil forecasting, a handling
of unanticipated magnetic fields realigning the world's most
rustic forces into ruined spheres utterly alien at their cores.
Soul-forging metallurgists shave
from a meteoroid's rind its abyssal trick,
its otherworldly earthlikeness the void polishes into
astral metal sheen—: bright filaments, serried debris from which they
melt, hammer, then cool an impeccable mineral edge
they will use to plunge straight to the center of the thickset,
geodetic heart of all matter. What
pyrogenic surplus of feeling frisks in the cast-off
of adamantine sediment scuffed
from that Promethean ore fire-engorged
with an axial energy everlasting? The forerunner
buries the fire the anteworldly sun unearths;
once incarnated, its lutred lore inscribes for ritual
embouchure's loveliest utterances:

myth.

Myth and song.

Helioastral Prometheus, whose Titanic style
connected antithetical realms—Star of the Sun, Fire of the Earth—
twice in matching wits with Zeus tricked the god
whose chariot drives the clouds that bellow over the plenteous earth. First
he took the lavish flesh and savory inners of an ox,
wrapping them in gauzy unappealing tripe; then
he took the chalky bones and smeared them
with fat, and then presented them to the god. Zeus,

sophical, vastagonal Zeus,

seeing through Ithax's ruse chose the bones nevertheless.
Because he planned sorrow and mischief against the men and women
Prometheus made from mud and loved. Because
he was loathsome and angry at heart and a god.
Because he saw everything, and because the tribes of men and women to
    this day burn
the white bones of decent creatures to the deathless gods upon their
fragrant altars buttered with gleaming, oleoresinous fat.

Furthermore, Zeus, high-thundering Son of Time,
kept from men and women the everlasting fire Prometheus

stole from him, hiding it in a hollowed-out fennel-stalk, huffing it
repeatedly to life as he crossed vast Attic distances
to bring it to them. *Pyrphoros*. Moving fire back and forth—thought itself.

Prometheus' gift of fire was stolen from the earth's unsleeping mood, its
tone of feeling roused by that recalescent theft Olympus anxiously
warded against, warred for, mercilessly penalizing the act of. The mind's
gnarled flame ignited. The earth's unconscious pooled, fluvial.

The little flint of glory. A rueful punishable deed. A little strange vibration.

And an eagle tearing at the umber of Prometheus' liver,
swollen with serums his anteolympian body outlives.

It's a carrion feeder. A darkness feeder. A fire wound.

Thought—divinity's precursor—lights up, fans out, roaring
pyrocumular waves across inclosing animations the mind
repeatedly harbors and flares forward.

                              In Mary's crimson robes her marrow surges
into the flaming branches of the Burning Bush a fire holier
for drawing from earth's febrile roots life's tender, melancholic ransom
even orant, interceding Mary, fully enveloped in flames,
can't account for, her face a placid unscorched glare

the phlogiston she incarnates—an acheiropoetic firework
the *nomina sacra* abbreviates from eternity into time—
meteorically singes into image: abiding, rueful, overarching,

rare.

: :

Myth is the narrative metaphor sounds out of melodies
ideas finely tune in consciousness. Icons
carved from a ceaseless noise of thinking. The golden hissing notes inside them.

Why does it perceive these sensations? For it has daggered the crown of the sun.
Why does it stick to the light? For the soul is an extrusion of resins.
Why does it stink of this rottenness? For *the language of God has no grammar;*
   it consists only of names.
Why does it father what is merciful? For its athanatopsis is an autarchy.
Why does it mimic knaving wrens? For it changes darkness into light in
   matutinal song.
Why does its pressure flash awareness? For its textures are those of ice or cloth.
Why does it make this dazzling sign? For the books it wants aren't yet written.
Why does it work itself in friendship? For the Eleontic Primordium is the arena
   of life.
Why is it always current and ancient both? For I live in it.
Why is it mistaking despair for depression? For the seasons, one after another,
   draw out like a music the feeling.

Why is it so conformed to this world? For to be transformed by the renewal
   of your mind
is to be changed in your shape.
Exteriority. Interiority. Ascent.

Why is it a dream-power every night showing thee thine own? *For a man is*
   the conductor of the whole
river of electricity.

   — : —

When the river plain was prairie
when the riverslope inclined to the plane of the horizon
when the riverlings riffling into the floodplain were gushing
when the convergence of wet system with hurricane rushed up the
   Midwestern summertime
when the rain for two days straight came down
when the *shamanistic shuddering-shouting awakened something real in the depths of our*
   native poetic sound
when the rivermeadow under dilations of stillicidous indraughts flushed
when the valves of the land busted open—
there was a bore
a confluence
a rainy swash: a flood.
September 13th and 14th, 2008, in Riverside, in Lyons, the Des Plaines
breaching its banks.

A functional river ecosystem is connected to everything around it.

Sodden basement garbage.
Migrating fall-time birds.
Junky fisherman minding the morning.

Afterwards, its waters retreated: the floodplain's flora felted with muddy
    ash everywhere. Plovers
cherrypicking minute crawdads, stranded mudpuppies in isolated puddles
in the woods, along the rivercourse.
Plastic tatters of sandbags two meters up, bewitched in ragged scrub:
    how many
years will it take to clear this already shabby
forest preserve of new debris?
Little solemn disaster. Little *nothing really* that happened.
Little curdled spume caught in the loggy cluster
snagged by a bank.

Strange holy enclosing scene fluming turbidly out—
The exaltation, not merely the conversation, of the elements by convergence.

The exaltation, not merely the pituitous riverine wax
the convergence, not entirely the bizarre essence
the gift, not only the benefit, not only the blessing song
the kiss, not everywhere the touch
the acid, not implicitly corrosive

the nucleation, the horde of living tissue

inertia, not automatically expanding

negation, not retracting as expected, not immediately so

the glory, and its correlate confusion

the rule-breaking restlessness, a way of entering in:

the mysteries of the ecology, the environment knowing itself:

the surprising patterns of its parts.

I find a snake writhing upstream in the gushers—a pet set free by the storm?

I find woodpeckers, robins, blue jays thriving in the woods.

I find rivers of thought, waxy in semiliquid aspic, surging hilariously forth.

I find I incorporate arterial profluences as well as

problems of navigation.

I find the riverhead, the river dragon, the river terraces metaphysical comforts

    for the uncertainties

about the precise qualities of the chemical composition

that make up the river's peculiar

amylaceous smell.

I find this river a bradyapneatic exhalation of a once healthy suspiring system.

I find the Des Plaines River to be urban planning's lost forethought.

Its Promethean western barrier.

I find the river, done with flooding, following its brumous way

through a series of seedy woods.

I find the water a lactiferous brown.

I find it a sudsing barm.

I find it warm and gelatine.

I find it daily gurgling.

I find it circulating through the world.

I find it streaming, I find it coursing, I find it in antic, manic flux.

I find it exuberant.

I find it spurred.

I find it undrinkable.

I find it full of flooding force.

I find it accidental.

I find it rebegun.

Concresced.

Perfectly disturbed, a drifting

pathway for all the birds.

: :

of the erth, erthy
as we have borne the ymage off the erthy

Said God: a heifer, a she-goat, a ram three years old apiece.

A turtledove and a pigeon. And he knew and he split them each

up the middle placing the halves each apart from the other

but not the birds—these he kept uncut. And birds of prey

aggressively coming down, winged jaws, tooth of sky,

so Abraham took the carcasses and stored them—*Arcanum*

of sunlight in which they sizzled, cured—God-denying

betrayal of the sun setting burning slowly into the sand,

sinking redness into the earth; and awareness,

a ghost of deep sleep coming down on him and here

huge terror coming over him, shadow and horror.

And the sun setting and the darkness, the *caligo tenebrosa,*

the thick and dazzling darkness, the oven of fuming smoke,

the flaming lamp of fire, spooky movement in the noctuary,

the sacred solace of the altared night. What are the lights

that hover in sleep? And what kind of god requires all this sacrifice from us?

    : :

Uniform in loneliness

hieroglyphic in mystery, holographic in aspect, as much psychic projection

    as fleshly fact—

Only in the little dawn beginning things, only in

the lull the air pulls from the last sweet urges to keep sleeping, only in the

    morning's all-holy mouth

I like

the lull light makes you wake with, resonant

of your pulsating birth-star, an eccentric ledge mender,

valved with light,
voice of dawn,

voice of morning,
voice of day's beginning—

hankering, anxious intensifications en-
gross the morning's pathic massiveness, that
mystical aptitude
nude in the runaway light

I register in the way the palm warblers spill through the woods' lower stratum
believing in my soul
in the migratory pattern they flash into the world
you summon
my imagination to recognize—a magnetic map the
soul traverses in somatic appulsion from body to body, creature to creature
    incandescing.

Immortal.
Fathomless.
Onward and outward.
The float and odor of hair.
The thoughtful merge.

   — : —

Differentiation. Autopoeisis. Communion.

Energy's copulating androgyne.

Radiant structures of the animate world.

Resistance. Force. Dreams.

Autofellation. The surge and the need. The vaginal twitter.

Beatitude of reading; beatitude of the love embrace, the sexual evening, its
    anticipated lateness.

The thermonuclear sustenance of the sun.

The ongoing collapse of our galactic cloud.

Thought's self-imploding centers.

The universe is a single multiform development

in the kaleidoscopic quantum

vacuum

of human

reverie.

Its particulate Himalayan effluvium—stone

molten into time. Yogic

domestication of the breath. Love's

percussion, honey, disoxygenating

fury. That centripetal feeling coming on,

sweetness coming on, that

theocentric order and ornament.

  : :

Make holy

all you works of God with praise and exultation

you angels of God and you heavens, you magnifiers of all the single quantum's
original energy

you hydrogen and helium, you universe of frenzied particles billowing out

you primordial billion years depthless night shuddered toward transfiguration
through

you praise, you magnification

you unbearable creative moment

you consuming sacrificial force;

make holy

you galactic internal dynamics, you spew of stars, you luminous intensities

you waters coursing over heaven and you dynamos generating their power

you slow-burning yellow star

you socket of life

you Sun and Moon

you same sized argentine luminaries drifting in the skies

you fungal spores into the sinuses huffed

you wicked lunar eclipse

you dais of cooling light years;

make holy this song by blessing, by building up with praises

you telescope of time, you notion of creation

you most antique ledge of energy it peers toward

you aeonic disdain, you horror torus

you flowing forms, you atmospheric womb, you cellular chemistries, you
earthly life

you showers and dew, you souls

you tenderly dusted, glimmering mineral energy wound

you little animations of things

you prokaryotic cells, you knitters together, you fashioners of life

make holy this song

by filling your chemical bellies with food from the sun

by binding packets of bright particles sped down to the brooding earth

with data of the life mass

and make holy

you fires, you heat, you winters, you hot summers

you dews and dendritic frosts

you icy rimes and you polar colds

and you praisers and exalters, you oxygen saturating earth's system

you environmental instability, you cosmic burning aspect

you firestarters, you setters ablaze of things

you oxygen-devouring eukaryotic cells

you sweet fuckers

you meiotic, gametic procreant urge

you involuntary erections and you sexual daytime

you avid winter ice and you fluffy winter snows

you days and nights passing through them

you light

you gloomy darkness

you bottom-down sadness sadder still

you exfulgurations and you clouds

you rapid hapless scattering of electricity;

make holy this song

you multicellular forms, you bodies, you polyps, you worms, you insects, you
    clams, you sponges,

you spiders, you leeches, you backbones

you lifeforms

surging, metabolizing, expiring

you corpses, you spent energy, you unspooling tendrils of mushroom protein

you anuses extruding that vitalizing hash

you necrophagous moonlight fruits

you eaters of your own dead and you living things

you caloric scavengers and you sex scroungers;

make holy this song

you fountains gushing up and you seas and flumes

you rivers flowing

you sad sewage foaming and you amylaceous wastes curdling

you tannic yeasty odor

and you passerines migrating through the leaves oxygenating the reek

you hydrodynamic, pluvious Des Plaines

you lather at the turbine falls

you guggled twitching spent alongside;

make holy this song

you mammals

you new emotional sensations

you intoxicated central nervous system

you flowers displaying and you pollenators

you songbirds in sexual colors

and you flesh of fruit

and you mother and baby sensing the quality of these things and
     remembering it

you elephantine-massive whales and whatever else in the waters moveth

you birds of the sky threading the air with flight

you innovation of flying

you lumbering beasts of the land

you cattle sweet as grass

and you handsome cougar slain in the neighborhood

and you little housecat sphinxes perplexing the sun

you peoples

you daughters and you sons;

make holy this song

you quadripedal hand freed from the task of walking

you eye seeing it flex

you sweet liquor of light and rain falling down

you mind imagining this

you sweet interiors

by magnifying the moment

by corroding the pathways that internal vision followed

by decaying the mind toward morbid presciences imagination fecundates;

make holy this song

you trillions of neurons keeping the creature

you stellar vistas of cells

you epiphenomenal loop

you initial leap from action to reflection, from pathway to memory

you self-thought, you slot of distinction, you crashed acid and
   phosphorescent flare

you infancy, you chance to learn, you curious sexual forms

you *phallic thumb of love*

and you *thruster holding me tight*

you pressure in the uterine clutch, you glare of the rich palpation, you
   proposition of sperm

you orchid boat and you winged serpent

you sweet sleepiness

you relaxed body

you nations of the world

you language coming in and you priests serving God

you spirits, you souls, you depths, you justice

you holiness, you humble heart;

make this song holy

you excentrations of life, you lutrescent syrup in the veins

you autochthonomous animal forms shifting pneumatic, imaginal shape

by numerously erupting with fire

by impulsively giving birth

by catastrophically sanctifying the metaphors

by interpenetrating the coital cluster

by singing out *love's ancient evidence*

by haplessly magnifying the glassy melancholic interiors

by warding us with charms

by stitching us alphabetic talismans from strands of DNA

by forming tissue from moon spores and rubber

by leading us on

by thinking

by praising and exalting the Lord forever.

If you abolish the symbols, then you tear down the walls of your own house.

You should unfold the core of the symbols—
We are the questions.

So praise.

Ananias, Azarias, Misael.

Bless the Lord. Praise and exalt him forever.

    : :

What is this fearsome mystery fulfilling itself in me?

What is this mind seeing invisible unornamented formless shapes?

What is this earthy fire lathered in its hearth's outlandish ore?

Who is this homicidal dragon glaring brilliantine in the hellish cosmic genesis?

What is this oracle bodied forth in me daily?

Who the bride and who the bridegroom secretly joined?

What is this humantic sphere, this lumen, yes, this flame?

— : —

Avid explosions of migrating warblers
bursting in patterns in woodlands and prairies,
suburbs and flyways they zodiac with symbols
predicting our thinking. Chromatic bodies

light pressure mirrors from solar antonyms
transforming cardinal time into vernal lusts—
nesting defenders, selective aspirers speciate
properties air draws from time's distilling gravities.

Lustred migrations. At every hour we've ever imagined, a bird is on the
    wing: a robin
keeping pace with the melting edge of snow cover; a whooping crane's
    dramatic solitary fanning
in a streak of sandhills; an arctic tern jetting
from pole to pole in a vast seasonal circuit; an indigo bunting finding
the border zone where woodland opens into clearing; a ruby-throated
    hummingbird
purring across five-hundred miles of coastline on a gram
of nectar. Relentless nights and days of movement.
Survival's ancient itch only arrowing onward scratches. The mind's
a migratory evidence, the projection of the human animal's consciousness
from instinctive enclosures of neural circuits fired with latent gifts to the
    dynamiting

outer expanding world: our first depictions
were animals—bulls, gazelles, cranes, souls.

Migration's astonishing parallels between image and idea, between
species and soul in communion with motion, in
commotion, its eucharistic transformations:
a brown creeper and two golden-crowned kinglets
in the stardowned snowfall
of an April's unwarranted weather
migration seethes northward through in spite of
the season's agitations. The little puff of pressure signaling
a Wilson warbler's passage through the birch tree's
new leaves.

       Three splendidly yellowing magnolia warblers
uplifting through a maple tree.
Hermit thrushes' spooking ghostflow through the underbrush.
Flocked starlings' geometric detonations
inspired like fireworks. Migration's notes:
the woods' logophragous originator, *song*. It is
creation's symphonic dilator, birds' iconic identifier:
pluck of notes and the riverine sillage. Stillness as an energy.
Woods swarmed with palm warblers, with flashes of yellow-rumped
warblers. Elementalism of cool light, palely cloud-filtered.
Disastrous trashing of the paths of the woods.

These sweet woods provide cover for evolution's outlandish

artificers, song-crowned, crowned in song.

Perception's filtration system: ricocheting catalogues of unruly song, territorial
   call:

it's spring's brand-new body making noise.

Orange peels, bait trays, charred plywood, broken malt-liquor bottles,

the turgid Des Plaines guzzling by. Sunlight

expressing greens. Sponge of wood, soft decay, kneeling deer.

Reefs of mushroom glazed with vernal liquor. Thrush songs three-dimensional.

In alchemy, the wren who vexed Thoth.

In admixture, the summer terns with segmented wings and the patterned earth.

In sunlight, the ensouling over the forest.

In doctrine, metempsychosis.

In practice, the transmigratory elaborations, the little autochthonomous soul
   leavings.

In evenings, the firefly's transmigratory dynamo,

the firefly's renewed lutrescent fuse,

that little phosphorescent flare of transanimation.

In prayer, the little struggles, the pressing awareness of flaws.

In the world, ongoing wars,

the sadness of foolishness.

In actuality, grace. Life from life—the vital force burst through the body's
   feathers.

In flight, birds. Arrowing off the earth.

Eleuthera. January. Bahamian berries

sweeten slowly over the winter season but March

is arid and the berries grow scarce. The island's scrub

secretes afflicted woodland warblers whose

rapid wintering movements researchers

track in twenty-one day stretches accomplished by

tiny radio transmitters a half-gram heavy

one angel-hair wisp of antenna extends from

held

to the body

of the bird

with two

cotton

strings.

        Each

chipper

broadcasts its own

frequency.

Kirtland's warbler, rare

as air on Mercury. The little phoenix fledged from fires

burned through stands of jack pines stretched

between Grayling and Mio. Northern Michigan. Its last remaining habitat.

Entirely managed. Little fickle specialist. Its

only nest in the bottom branches of a jack pine no more
than five years old. How can the bird survive?
Woodland warbler. Forest fire thriver. No more woods.
No more fires. Black lores cleaving a gray cowl. Rainy day spotting him.
Gay speckled yellow on the breast. The largest
of the North American warblers. Nearly wiped out.

Pyxgeau is their lord, a
twenty-five-thousand-mile traveler, nine years old
banded by researchers as a fledgling then repeatedly rebanded
over the years, first purple, then yellow, then aluminum, then green,
    then orange,
blue-gray feathers his Odyssean oars, native
Michigander, bearer of migratory symbols zoodelic pathways
reveal in air to be the patterns of consciousness
recognized in its deepest retinal self—. Little
latter-day survivor. Little memory remnant of the forest world.
Little once-abundant mystery streamer.
                                Little prodigious
migrator. Little signaler of the end of days.

  : :

The ghost's lonely hours. In them.
It's sweet. Going in the sun.

The walls summer yellows.
The soft hiss of footfalls the grass ruffles out.
Pan's son. Slept into marble. Gray.

Drunk on brown wine, evenings.
Peach in the leaves. Its glow. Its splendid redness.
A Joplinesque sonata. Laughter.
Lifting up from the cellar.

The night's sweet silence.
The dark plains where shepherds coalesce
white stars. From mercury.

Autumn.
Charity in the grove. Melancholic hours.
Red walls we wander along. That calm. That
lucid calm. Birds that curve into our eyes.
Nightfall. Funeral jars the white waters sink through.

Ecstatic gymnastics heaven in bare branches practices.
Bread and wine the grass farmer bears. His open hands.
Fruits in the cellar. Ripening sweetly.

The dead. Their earnest looks
the soul savors
like a greeting.

Brute quiet of wasted gardens.

The novice there, the brows he garlands with browning laurels.

The icy gold his exhalations plume around.

Bluish waters those hands disrupt.

Or the white cheeks of the sisters. In the cold night.

Sweet and easy: a stroll past friendly living rooms.

Where there's solitude. Where the maples sift the winds in hisses.

Where the thrush sings. A territorial hymn.

A man is a beautiful thing. Shining in darkness.

Arms and legs moving. Astonishing. These swings.

Eyes—their purple sockets. Swiveling in silence.

Vespers. The little stranger. November's destroyed era he's lost in.

A sacred grove's rotted branchwork, leprous walls enclosing.

Where the holy brother used to wander

sunk in the soft pulsations of his madness.

Lonely last gasps of the evening wind.

Bowed head in the gloom of the olive trees. That fading

image.

Seismic, the generation's worsening.

The gazer's eyes filling with the gold of his stars.

At this hour.

Evening. Bells—never again to sound out—fading.
Ruination of the black walls of the square.
Sound of the dead soldier called to prayer.

An angel. Bleached. Etiolated.
A son sets foot in the empty house of his father.

All the sisters have gone away to white old men.
The sleepers found them under the columns of the alcove. In the night.
Returned from sad pilgrimages.

Shit and worms clotting their hair.
There. The sleeper's silver feet. The dead
toneless steps he takes from empty room to empty room.

You psalms. In fiery midnight downpours.
There. Servants thrashing eyes with stinging nettles.
An elderberry's sweet little fruits.
Dangling over an empty grave.

Lemoning moon. Rolling easily.
Across a young man's fever linens.
Followed by winter's silence.

Lofty destiny brooding over Kidron.

A cedar, that lovely creature
spreading out beneath the blue glare of the father.

Nights a shepherd leads his flock across an open field.
Or there are cries in the zero of sleep.
Or in the sacred grove an adamantine angel comes upon a man.
And the flesh of the holy ones melts away on the glowing racks.

Purple vines entangling huts of clay.
Argillaceous bundles of yellow corn.
Drone of bees. Flight of cranes.
Evenings. When the resurrected meet on mountain paths.

Lepers reflected in black waters.
Or opening the shit-shotten robes.
Weeping. To the balsam of the wind. The rose hill scented in it.

Skinny girls. Touching their way through the streets of night.
Looking for the loving shepherd.
Saturdays—the sweet singing from the houses.

Let that song be about the boy.
About his madness. About his shining brow. About him going.
So sad to see him again.

Madness. Its hues. In black rooms.
Shadows of old men under open doors.
Helian's soul there, looking at itself, in the rosy mirror.
Snow. Leprosy. Falling from his brow.

On the walls the stars all fizzled out.
All the white shapes of the light.

Bones in the graves arising. From the tapestry.
Ruined crosses—their silence.
Sweet incense in the purple night wind.

You crushed eyes. In black mouths.
Grandson in gentle dementia.

Alone. Contemplating the darker ending.
Silent God closing blue
luminescent eyelids over him.

  : :

We learned to like the Fire

Zeros. Phosphoros—Glaciers.
The Wizard Sun.

Nerve, grave, Poltroon, Oxygen, Circuit, Circumference.
Murmuring, inner than bone, Knots of Apparitions, Horror, Torment,
a Spotted World, Suns, Deforming, Dwindling, Gulphing up,
Earths, Firmaments, Cram, Velvet Head, "Sip, Goblin," Arctic Creatures,
Adamant, Amber shoe, fair fictitious People, Blesseder
Ground, or Air, or Ought:
Freight.

Somewhere, then, there is a transformation . . .
The question is, *where*—in the nerve world or in the mind world.

— : —

Out of the magnetic massings
out of the feeling of the season lifting
out of the cloud of forgetting and unknowing
out of the woolpack and the fair weather days of air in the clear
out of the soft cloudiness of afternoon napping and
out of the avid energy

out of an absolutely *original center*
in which the universe reflects itself in a unique and inimitable way:

the exaltation and not merely the convergence.

Cloud.

Cloud around which all darkness gathers

cloud into which each secret thing is hidden

cloud from which the prism casts its opaque forgetting

cloud through which the Mosaic sojourner stutteringly backs

cloud: profluent, shadow-glutted cloud:

unutterable gift of grace,

noctivagitous matter of praise and attention

ancient fathers brought together out of the impossibility of constant
    wakefulness;

cloud out of which the marvelous beguiler draws lurid shapes:

Cloud: I bid you hide from God

the crude

desire of your heart

the breathed holy head

the gaping mouths

the solely fuller heavenly holy

error alone

in

pitchy, sombrous clouds

overhead.

To the immense point where earth from space is seen I came: eyes'

slivered lunulae tilting toward it. The great land unknown

below me; the seething seas. Potent feelings of openness.
Sad and aching planet. *The fibrous roots of every heart*
on earth infix'd deep in its restless twists. Impossible
profusion of souls; ferrous reinforcement of time. Sun's
witnessing mass. Pneuma's unruly numen. *Lord.*

Fear's reef of soma.
World: fundamentally and initially living. Essentially kinetic.
Its life: one vast psychic operation.
Great flame leaping out.
Sonorous arson roaring worldwide: fires of seas, great stained atmosphere,
meteoric cataclysm civilization slowly is.
Clouds. Solid
clouds rain
like vinegar from a sponge
is squeezed from
dripping
down
to earth.

   : :

Sister Moon.

You have this feeling that this thing is alive.
76 million pounds of thrust.

A strange silence;

purled implosion billowing flame—
holocaust of rocketing smoke:

gravity's inverse is fire.
It feels just like it sounds. To feel all the power precisely
directed. At last; I'm leaving earth and I'm destined for the moon.

New moon.
Moon sickness.
Moon wolf.
Tincture from which all the dead are revived.
Tincture of the first-created ferment.
Flower and fruit of all light.
Whitening illuminator.
Autochthonomous fossil.

There are no boundaries to what you are seeing.
Halleluiah.
25,000 miles an hour.
You're the representative of humanity at that point in history.
If there's anything remorseful about going to the moon, it's
that you don't get enough time to spend
around the earth.

Translunar injection burn.

30,000 feet per second.

You have to see this planet to believe it.
Wandering star.

People. Green trees. Fresh water.
The earth
from here
is a grand
oasis in the great
vastness

of space.

> Womanly and gentle star.
> Moon marriage.
> Mother of the sun.
> Vessel of the sun.
> *Infundibulum terrae*—funnel of the earth—receiving
> and pouring out the powers of heaven.
> Moisture of the moon.
> Lunar humour.
> Silver alchemist, its synonymous Arcanum.

Holy promise of the *plenilunium.*
Rabid dog, divine child, waxing mediatrix of the whitening of the
    inner world.

Do you really know where you are in this time and in this space, actually?
When sunlight
shines through the blackness of space, it's black.
But I can see it.

It's not a hostile blackness. Welcome
to the moon's sphere. You're in
the influx. After passing nothing, you're in the presence
of the moon.

    Ecclesiastical moondew.
    Silverine sap of life in secretion.
    Moon ichor. Philosophical ablution.
    Bride and bridegroom.
    Health and sickness.
    Metallic moon-roots of red-stemmed, black-veined flowers.
    Salty fountain, sweetness of sages.
    Sponges in the lunar sea.
    Blood and sentience.

You're in the presence of some law, some
presentiment of an all-energizing

memory.

It gave one the feeling of foreboding.

You're drifting into the shadow.

This is not real. You're back in the stimulator.

To make mankind something different than it was.

Bringing back thought and feeling as important as bringing back a rock.

To stand in Taurus-Littrow.

Brighter sun, blacker sky.

Brilliantly illuminated earth.

The path of evolution is now in space.

The curve of human evolution has been bent.

A spiritual presence—earth's attention focused.

Adam. Or Eve.

Alone. With that special communication.

We felt an unseen love.

The moon is different.

Moon plant. Mandrake. Lunetica. Tree of the Sea.

Mind of the whole.

Great luminous thought. Nighttime fungus.

Spherical soul. Globe of the moon.

Soror. Mater. Uxor.

Sister-wife. Initiatic dragon. Arsenic transfigurer.

Mother-beloved.

Unworldly world.
Shimmerer of Eros.
Moonlight from a full moon.
Unseen love. Inner life.

: :

The world assumes an outward air
it strobes with light it cannot bear
while inside nurtured brightness dims
the visions conjured in its hymns.

What sickness measures forms in thought
a light into whose background fraught
intentions bring unchecked decay:
the source—

        an earthen corpse—

                on which we pray.

— : —

Cuneal wren.
Botryoidal mind.
Vine of thoughts, branching imagination—
flurried termini of nervous signals. Profound tune. Sweet deep song in
    the throat.

Saint in tatters
of gold—elongated and elucidated. Glorious incarnation
the mind's bird form fixates
in hurried speech, in trilled scales of ceaseless thinking
dream unechoes into ballooning drone
syrup stores in the mental apiary's vastagonal casks
the overarching oracle of sleep
magnetizes, phyletizes:

the forms have evolved
the body is all

It's the wren that vexed Thoth:

the slain wren
the golden-crested wren
the hunted wren
the little king
the father's murderer
God's sparrow
the prophetic bird
the ornithological fact
the halcyon myth
the floating nest
the vivid plumage
plunged into the sea

the king of trees

the soul of the oak

the copper-feathered pheasant

the hornet-headed drake

the wind-colored snipe

the crimson-hooked gull

the awkward young hawk

the azimuth of thrush

the terror-glossy crow

the wren in the central place

the starlings in twirling squadrons

the archaenoetic cranes

the fattening hens

the unabashed chickadee

the sepulchral swans

the slaughterous rookery

the autarchic bird lord

the pleromatic fixation

the autistic nucleus

the Canaanite mythology

the silly Celtic lore

the centroverted formation

the ocean of Godhead

the self-re-entrant pathology

the life-spanning midst

the cannibalism

the sorceress who transforms men into animals

the firmamentally liberating act

the inner voice

Here's the fable: all the birds are gathered together
to decide which is the greatest of the birds and deserves
therefore to be king. *Whichever flies farthest*, the cranes
and terns submit. *Whoever lives longest*, the ostriches say.
Whichever are most splendid, say the peacocks fanning
their tail feathers and say as well the birds of paradise
radiantly iridescing. *No, whichever sings most beautifully*,
say the brown thrashers on behalf of the hermit thrushes,
too shy to sing for themselves. *Whoever flies highest*,
says the golden eagle, lunging forward. But as he plunges
upward into the air, the little house wren unseen, his tail feathers
bent to jut up, hops into the feathers on the golden eagle's ruff
and clings there as the eagle's pinion muscles work
to oar up into the sky.   At the upper nearly airless arch
of his flight, the eagle declares, "There, I'm nearly
into space itself, king of all below," and begins to tilt,
dropping back down to earth but not before feeling
the little pinch of the wren leaping up and hearing
the rapid purr of his tiny cinnamon wings battering

what little air is there and pronouncing,
"Thou hast not outflown me;
I am king of all I see
and cleverer than I am free."

Now here's the thing: the eagle is life itself, its
striving vital force always upward gaining,
always finally tiring. So what's the wren? The mind's feeling force—
the heavenly starlight that shines unwaning.

: :

Thunder-uttered Theban earth. Autochthonomous kratophany. Lutrid
    New God.
Midwived by lightning fire. Divine skin sloughed.
To be in this human one. On the banks of these two rivers in the land.
Where evidence of God's arson scars my slain mother.
Where God's fire lurches upward living.
God's wife's crime.
Her vengeance. Her violence.
This place blest I've blessed again.
With grapevines. Pendulous with fruit. All around.
Persia—its solar terraces. Bactria—its battlements. *Chthonos.* The earth,
itself. Medes—that nastiness.

Arabia—prosperity. A sea of brine laps the bright beaches
stretching from Galatia to Greece; from rude
anchoritic cells to bright Aegean towers:
Barbarians and Greeks.
Brought together.

And I'm back: daemonic Bromios. Disruptor of
earth's sacrament: life. In Greece. I'm back.
Having orgiated Afghanistan.
And Ethiopia. And Arabia. Where the wealth
streams even in crude rivers. That I'm God.
And I'm here. Thebes.

Whose horrors my presence amplifies as lies and frantic errors.
In fawnskin. I have clothed the wailing women.
Thyrsus is thus: more missile than staff.

My mother's betrayers. Her sisters: liars. Whores.
Of rumor. I've made them manic. Because of this. Stung their wits.
With agitation. Forced them. Into mountain wilderness.
Where they mince in farcical tatters—.
The lying ladies. Practicing
false bloodless rites:
communion with fame. Concerts with vanity.

And all the Cadmean women.

I've cursed them. With madness and driven them. From their homes.

This wretched empty city. Clever. Uninitiated. Unlearnèd.

Its cliffs tufted in fir trees.

Zeus. My father. And for my slandered mother

who bore me: as a god

—daemonic Bromios—

I come.

Mantled in the earth's rottenness, enunciated by its earthquake shibboleth,

opened by the mountains' even chorus, draped

in fawnskins, in filth, nude in moonlight, bloodthirsty

for the slain goat, the great skinned beeves, the cut doves, the eviscerated ocean fishes, their

roe rudely harvested, their carcasses discarded,

the glad meal of raw flesh,

great consumer of living forms, great god of these wanting systems of life:

witness for us the repetitious machinery of our making—

Bromios! Thunder-uttered. Seismoeidoloic theandron. New god for an old world.

Euhoi!

Welcome.

Milk. Wine. Nectar. Honey-blood.

Each thins. Each keeps thinning.

Torch of flaming pine.

Slag of coal.

Torched nuclear dynamo.

Wicked glut of calories.

Sweet smoke from Syrian incense.

Fennel wand inciting the gasping dancers, starved

for extra oxygen in the throngs—enervating the airs.

Dance with them Bromios, shake your luxurious locks at the runaway moon.

Say, "Onward and on

you insatiable sinners. Onward and on, you gold harvesters

and you money squanderers, you exploiters and usurers, you

fiends of coins."

Say, "My praises: sing.

My gravitous tympanum: rumble.

My ecstasy: titillate.

My earth fucking: enstasiate.

My lovely pipe: shrill on it.

My holiness: invoke.

My holy song: give glorious throat to.

My holy mountain: make the earth into.

My excavernous mining operation: fund it."

Like foals with their mare,

like anger with other passions,

the bacchanalian bellowers, these billions-crowded planet dwellers,

caterwaul and gambol

on nimble, nimble

legs.

Scorning fools. This new daemon. This divinity. The dynamogenic mass:
this potentate. This Lord of Greece.
This charism, this power. You can't even feel it.
He anoints the world with his fluid. Two vital principles.
He summons. And concentrates:
earth and ether. Earth was originally Demeter's: the goddess's grain.
Her nourishment. Her provisioning. Her furnishing
the people with bread. Ether is the vine's juice.
Intoxicating the body's moods. Its airs. Its despairs.
A young boy loggy with vine-must: Iaccus: he lords it,
he coaxes forgettance with fruit, fermentates it, musks it, seals it for mellowing,
letting men and women forget their griefs.
Misery's pharmacy—wine's draining.
This Lord of Greece is our new god the gods themselves
pour out in libations. His spirit's fluid. What blessings we win from
fickle gods we win from what ether
we pour onto the parching earth. Pneumatic man's thirsty earth.
Thunder-uttered, autochthonomous, lutrid New God. Ritual timbrels sounded.
Fawnskins donned. Dawn surpassed by fiery day.
Morsel of sky broken off, hostage of earth's contentiousness.
Goddess's avowing anger. New god midwived by lightning fire.
Daeomic skeptomancer—this god's also a prophet: mania
manifesting mantic powers evermore, and largely. Asynchronous,
forecasting aspect of the madness his divinity endowing us with sun
propels toward us. From the future. Where bellicose anticipations

trigger Pan's randomness: soldiers rowdy with fear as battle

approaches them. That's Bromios—thundering readiness. Mark these words:

you'll see him, if not now, then someday in eternity. Capering on the cliffs

    above Delphi.

Waving fuming pine torches. Brandishing that Bacchic wand. So, Pentheus:

rue-maker. Fool. Hear me: no king's power surpasses any human life's.

And humans embody divinity's holy ether like a catastrophe of weather,

an energy system's unsound expressions

wildly uttered in exfulgerating displays, in earth's vocal throatings.

Receive this new god into your land. Pour him libations. Join his ecstatic dance.

Witness his destructive justifications.

Let him crown your head with sprigs of pine.

    : :

        You find this mixture of thousands, beloved, this
         riot of flowers let loose, overwhelming

Thought's cascading signals
—pattern is a form of patron—
its degenerating element, its
tendency to torpor
its fresh light let
in through the window casement
through the living form the window
opens out to, the world's
budding centers:
thought's carry-fist
its carvist,
its little falconine developments,
its evolutionary companion
falcon and man
owl's onyx, air's
embouchure, fluting
witness on the wind
Mind's *witnessing moonpoison,*
no autonomous mistress

Words of the Laws of the Earth
words of chemiluminescence
words of phosphorescence
words of prophecy
words incomprehended
words of inconclusions
words of worry and shock
words of spent power
bioenergetic words
Words of Music
Words of Feebleness, Nausea
Sickness, Ennui, Repugnance, and the like
words of the autochthonomian
words of the wren seeker
words of the women as well as the men
words of the sickening circuit
words of energy, waste, gluttony
words of the dawn before the dew
words of the rival dawnsong

mind's enveloping horoscope of
modulating contact points,
correspondences of antinomes,
appulsions of zodiac force, little
witnessing destinies,
little paleontological
perceptions, fossil meanings,
proprioceptive cures,
autism circuits,
speaking before the world;
thought's vibrations
in the vocal chords
resonating its prophetic
yet-voiced chorusing
into the dome of the mind.
Messianic patterning ideal
of the imagination.
Extraordinary aspirant
renascent environment of the theosoph
relaxing in his castle.
Enochic, apotheotic ideal.
End.
End that spells.
Nature's teleomorph is humankind.
Its clever endshaper.

words of the slain sparrow
words of the skillful housecat
Words of brothers
and words of sisters too
words of like termini
words of shape and shapeshifting
words of final desolation
words of enactment
words of human art
words of people knowing each other
words of an interconnected system
words of a poisoned stream
words of polluted rivers
words of fungal networks
words of the active hierophany
words of grasses
of folds, of sinuses, of angelic intercessions
words of fruiting disobedience
words of inheritance
of brotherly love
words of enclosed systems opening out
words of enviable figures
words of great trees
words of the transformed revocation
words of the snow turf

Falcon hooded on his wrist.   words of the minimum
            The glory of the stars   words of the cogwheels
          is the beauty of heaven   words of the summer sun stain
               a glittering array   words of the predated mourning doves
       in the heights of the Lord.   words of the shrill blue jay
              A breviary's praise.   words of the antique biomass
        Thought's obsidian tablet.   words surpassing the human terminus
  Thought's wooden table carved   words of the biogenesis
               with Pali glyphs.   words of the emergent soul in the land
             Thought's offering   words of the mind's minus
          at that table, thought's   words of the crepitating insect mind
      fastness of divine powers.   words of the ant hatchery
        Thought's soma, its elixirs,   words of a collective sorrow
      tapped from extensive roots,   words of bitter musk
             its nourishing waters   words of *the worldwide festival of death*
          boiled into syrups.   words of parsley
        Thought's glassy nectars.   words of heart-shaped leaves
   Mind's nectarine drunkenness.   words of pale hibiscus blooms
      Mind's inherited alcohols.   words of a sense of destiny
         Its attestations. Its facts.   words of spearmint
           Its commanding designs.
  Thought's broken slivers of glass,   Words of who are you
              its mosaic patterns.   awaiting these evolutionary assertions
        Its Mosaic darkness—its
              thickness, its dazzle,   to illuminate the shadowy cores of you
its enveloping temperate arborescence.   in the new blueness of the world?

. . .

Countersinging wrens
mouse birds
whose sharp incessant sloganeering
announces active territory
in little troglodytic trills
trrrrrrrr
tea-kettle gnosis stitched
through the little woodland with polygynous song.

A wren in the underbrush choruses
his mind a lute
strung with eighty songs he sings
springtime day long and night through

wrenny pugilistic tunes of beauty
his nearby rival countersings to, imitating,
amplifying his rhapsodies
to lure what females lurk in the leafy,
woody green.

CODA

Wren.
Omen.

Troglodytic wren. Wren of the varied tune.
Little earth-bound wren.
Little hole-dwelling soul.
Wren-thin omen offered the world.
Your soul's little mineral mood.
Little soul of the body of the earth.
Little emerald murmur; little mineral myrrh.
The earth's self-borne law.
Its gravitous autochthonomy. Its beardedness.
Its leathery elementation. Its keen aquiline piggy-backing.
Its excessive tiny intelligence.

Consciousness, according to neuroscientists, is epiphenomenal. This means, depending on the story you follow, that when consciousness arose in evolution, it did so as an action corollary to the functions otherwise necessary to the brain. Put another way, neither your brain nor your body require your consciousness in order to function and survive. Consciousness, then, is a kind of overplus of mental meaning, an excessive superfluity. It's also the totality of what we consider in life forms to be worthwhile, from its seemingly smoothly shaped core to its manifesting fringes.

And so, consciousness resembles grace. Grace is God's free and forgiving self-communication that allows all living creatures to partake in God's love. By definition an excess, an overplus. St. Augustine taught that grace is necessary to heal and liberate the freedom at the core of humankind. Cannot consciousness, whose most useful instrument is the imagination, serve best as that healer, that liberator? Ronald Johnson taught me that the image for the imagination is the Burning Bush.

The great Jesuit mystic and paleontologist Pierre Teilhard de Chardin saw the mind as an incandescence, the culmination of psychical temperature that had been rising in the cellular world for more than 500 million years. He imagined a "majestic assembly of telluric layers" culminating in an outer layer on which the spark of consciousness, lit from the first moment of awareness, is the point of an ignition that quickly catches, roaring into a growing blaze "till finally the whole planet is covered with incandescence." He called this planetary thinking layer the *noosphere* (the sphere of the mind) and believed it to be visible from space. "And even today," he wrote in 1940, "to a Martian capable of analyzing sidereal radiations psychically no less than physically, the first characteristic of our planet would be, not the blue of the seas or the green of the forests, but the phosphorescence of thought."

Teilhard believed that the "Personal" and the "Universal," that is to say the creaturely and the divine, are growing in the same direction to "culminate simultaneously in each other" in a moment of complete illumination.

But what about our blue oceans? What about our green woods, our fields of agribusiness crops, our polluted river systems, our planet of rapidly vanishing species? How do we come to terms with the grace of consciousness in the face of these ruinations, small and large? Even as there's a magnificence in the manner Teilhard envisions to the imagination as it arises from the totality of life that precedes it, there's something inescapably tragic about the way we've handled the gift of consciousness.

The poem I set out to write acknowledges these contradictions but mixes that awareness with other invariable concerns: creative urges, the desire to explore, the coming and going of seasons, animal life. It tracks the whole cycle of creation, not chronologically but intuitively, episodically, through the figure of a little house wren, seen one day in the woods, and who quickly comes to be an emblem for the imagination inhabiting a shaky world, a kind of witness to its shakiness. As authors, in part, of the world we inhabit, we're obliged, in addition to trying to rectify problems we've created, to bear witness in the form of honest testimony to the declining powers of our days.

Two coinages are at the core of this poem. First is *lutrescent* (also *lutrescence* and *lutrid*), which combines light with putrescent to suggest light gone rotten. This is supersaturated illumination. If there is a phosphorescence of thought, then there must be a way to account for decaying, rotten thought. The other coinage is *autochthonomous*. This word slots into the center of *autochthonous*, which means "native born" but also "of the earth itself," the Greek word *nomos*, which means law. So: of the earth's own native law. Essentially, this is an adjective for evolution but evolution as if it were a theology.

This poem arose from walks in the Village of Lyons Forest Preserve along the Des Plaines River, which flows mostly north-south through the western suburbs of Chicago, and its neighboring banks in Riverside, Illinois. The Des Plaines reeks with human misuse and runs with a muddy silt. But it serves as a migratory flyway and the woods of the forest preserve have been my primary bird watching spot for over a decade. The poem began for me while tromping through these woods, regularly strewn with the trash of revelers and the debris that comes with periodic floodings when basements of nearby houses disgorge their contents. Even so, and in spite of this, the forest preserve, like others in the Forest Preserve District of Cook County, is a great and needed space, created in a moment of civic enlightenment, a bulwark against a nastier world just outside its limits. Let my poem in some small way be an acknowledgment and a belated offering of thanks to those who created these places—legislators, enthusiasts, and nature-lovers—over a century ago.

ACKNOWLEDGMENTS

Support for the writing of this poem was provided by an artist's fellowship from the Illinois Arts Council and a Grainger grant from the School of the Art Institute of Chicago. My gratitude.

Portions of this poem appeared in the following journals, both print and electronic: *American Poet*, *The Cultural Society*, *The Golden Handcuffs Review*, *Hambone*, *Mantis*, *The Marsh Hawk Review*, *The Modern Review*, *Occasional Religion*, and *Talisman*. A portion of the poem also appeared in *The Arcadia Project*, edited by Joshua Corey and G. C. Waldrep (Ahsahta Press, 2012). In 2009, two deluxe chapbooks including sections of the poem were published by micropresses: *Benedicite* by Answer Tag Home Press, edited by David Pavelich; and *Wren/ Omen* by Albion Books, edited by Brian Teare. Both editors are keeping the tradition alive with their beautiful books. My profound thanks to them.

The concluding epigraph comes from Thomas Meyer, *Staves Calends Legends* (Highlands, NC: Jargon Society, 1979), used with permission of the author.

Sections of the poem are translations or para-translations of certain texts crucial to its argument. These include Ovid's *Metamorphosis* 1:5–31, Genesis 15: 9–12, the *Benedicite* (a medieval Latin hymn), Georg Trakl's "Helian," and Euripides' *Bacchae* 1–54; 135–166; and 272–313. Other sections take elements of thought as well as vocabulary, and at times formal notions, from thinkers and poets important to the poem, including Teilhard de Chardin, William James,

Whitman, Saint Symeon the New Theologian, Dickinson, Blake, Gerald M. Edelman (neurobiologist), and Gregory Bateson (theorist). Other parts of the poem take material or quote directly from Helen Macdonald, *Falcon*, and the films *Into Great Silence*, directed by Philip Gröning, and *For All Mankind*, by Al Reinert. For reference, Des Plaines is pronounced "dess planes."

Some portions of the poem, when originally published, bore dedications to Pam Rehm (Prometheus section); Jeff Clark (Kirtland warbler section); and Nathaniel Tarn (lunar landing section). Other debts through whom, in whom, and with whom: the Hair Club and Bazaar, Michael Autrey, Zach Barocas, Devin Johnston, Steven Manuel, Michael O'Leary, Edgar Sanchez, and Lissa Wolsak. This poem emerged from conversations about the mystery of human consciousness with John Tipton, begun in 2005. It bears the marks of his inquisitive care at every turn.

IN KELLS' BOOK   THE INTERLACE

BORDERS UPON   GOD'S WORD

BIRDS QUADRUPEDS   ENTWINED

TIL TAIL TURNS WING   WING LEAF

PEN TENDRIL   SLOUGHING OFF A

PRIMAL DOOM   WRITHING THROUGH

THE FIELD AN ALPHABET WHOSE LEAVES

MY HEART A WREN ITS VOWELS INVENT

Thomas Meyer
Staves Calends Legends